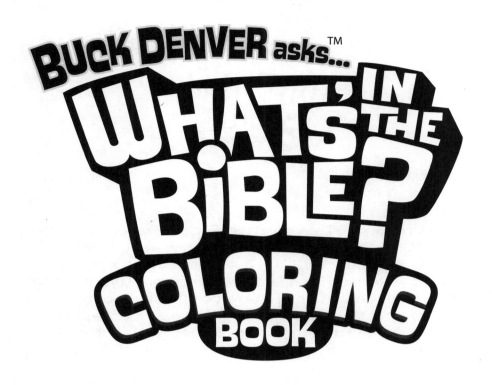

COLOR THROUGH THE BIBLE
FROM GENESIS TO REVELATION!

BASED ON THE DVD SERIES FROM
VEGGIETALES® CREATOR PHIL VISCHER

Brought to you from your friends at:

 **www.whatsinthebible.com**

TABLE of CONTENTS

The Old Testament

The New Testament

THE GOSPELS (MATTHEW - JOHN)

ACTS & PAUL'S LETTERS (ACTS - PHILEMON)

GENERAL EPISTLES & REVELATION (HEBREWS - REVELATION)

BONUS!

WHAT'S IN THE BIBLE? CHARACTERS

JELLYTELLY

THE OLD TESTAMENT

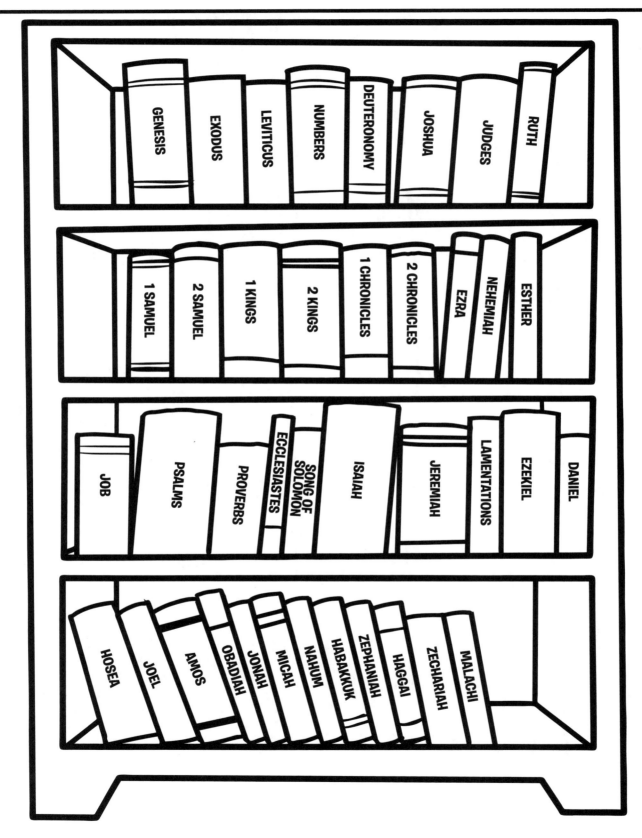

"In the beginning God created the heavens and the earth." Genesis 1:1

ALPHA

El Shaddai

Abba

GOD

YAHWEH

EVERLASTING FATHER

Jehovah-Jireh

Elohim

Adonai

Almighty

Jehovah

IN THE BEGINNING
Genesis

"The Lord God took the man and put him in the garden of Eden to work it and keep it." (Genesis 2:15)

God gave Adam and Eve a choice and they chose not to listen to God. God told them not to eat the fruit from the tree of knowledge of good and evil, but when the serpent tempted them, they ate the fruit. Sin entered the world. (Genesis 3:1-7)

Sin cannot be near God. When Adam and Eve sinned, they had to leave the Garden of Eden. (Genesis 3)

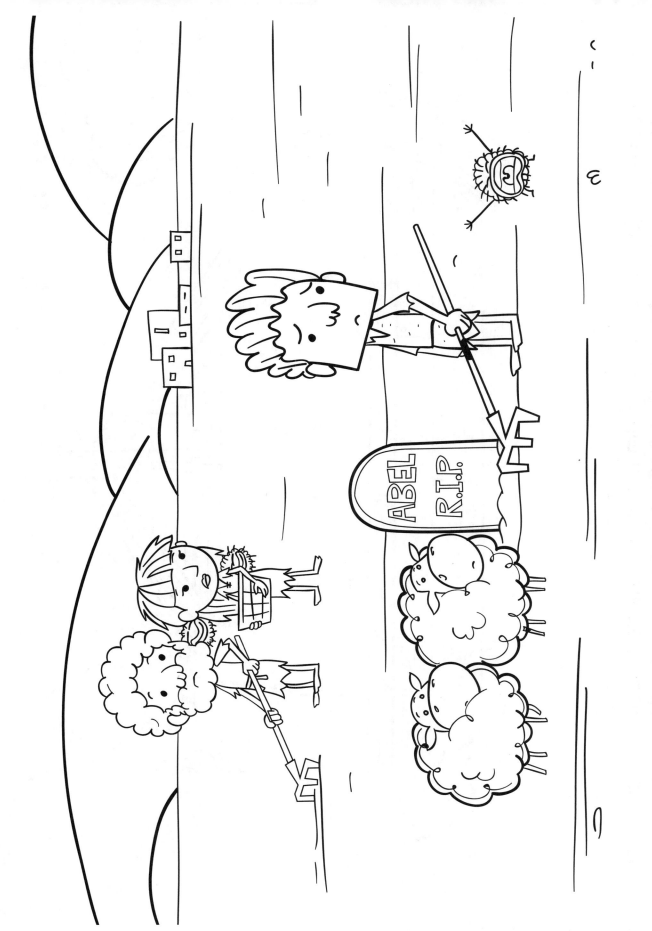

Sin spread. One of Adam and Eve's sons, Cain, killed his own brother, Abel. (Genesis 4)

God flooded the world because it was full of sin, but he chose one righteous man - Noah - to save. Noah and his family built an ark to withstand the flood, and they took two of every kind of animal with them on the ark. (Genesis 6)

Many years after the great flood, the people decided to build a tower so tall it could reach to the heavens! This was the Tower of Babel. God came down and saw the peoples' pride, and scrambled their language and scattered them across the earth. (Genesis 11:1-9)

Abraham was the first patriarch. "No longer shall your name be called Abram, but your name shall be Abraham, for I have made you the father of a multitude of nations." (Genesis 17:5)

ABRAHAM
(FATHER OF MANY)

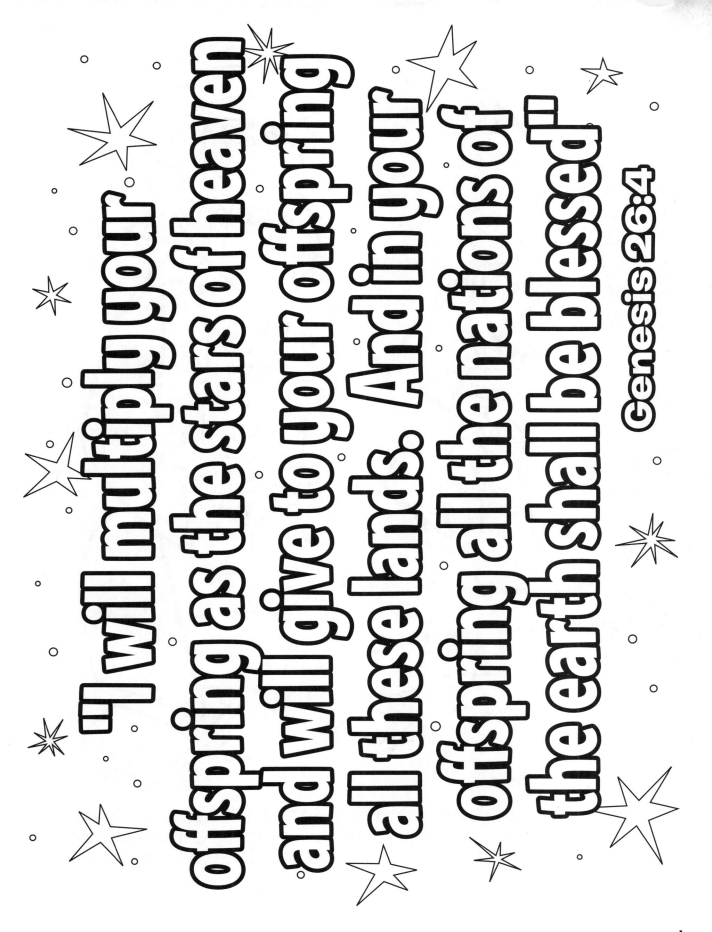

"I will multiply your offspring as the stars of heaven and will give to your offspring all these lands. And in your offspring all the nations of the earth shall be blessed" Genesis 26:4

Abraham and his wife Sarah wanted to have a baby, but they were very old and had never had one. But God promised Abraham he would have a son, and through him the whole world would be blessed. Then Sarah gave birth to Isaac! (Genesis 21)

God tested Abraham to see if he would give up everything for God – even his son! But at the last minute, God provided a ram for Abraham to sacrifice instead. (Genesis 22)

Isaac's son Jacob had 12 sons – including his favorite, Joseph. Joseph had a beautiful rainbow coat! One day his jealous brothers sold him into slavery. (Genesis 37)

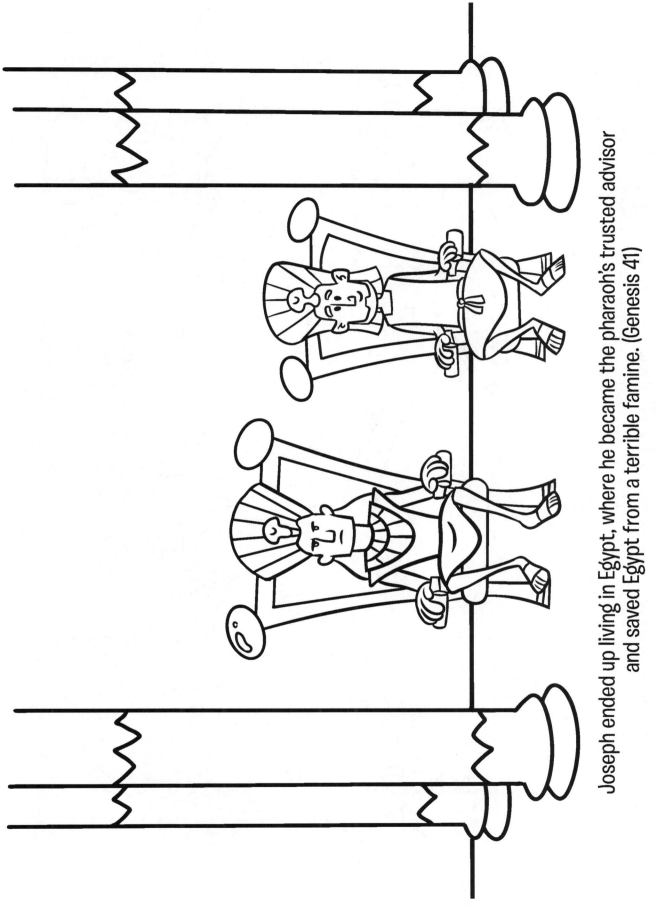

Joseph ended up living in Egypt, where he became the pharaoh's trusted advisor and saved Egypt from a terrible famine. (Genesis 41)

During the famine, Joseph's family came to Egypt to find food. Joseph revealed himself to his brothers and his father and promised to take care of them! (Genesis 45-46)

LET MY PEOPLE GO!
Exodus

The Israelites in Egypt were persecuted by the pharaoh. To save her son's life, Moses' mother put him in a basket and sent him down the river. (Exodus 2)

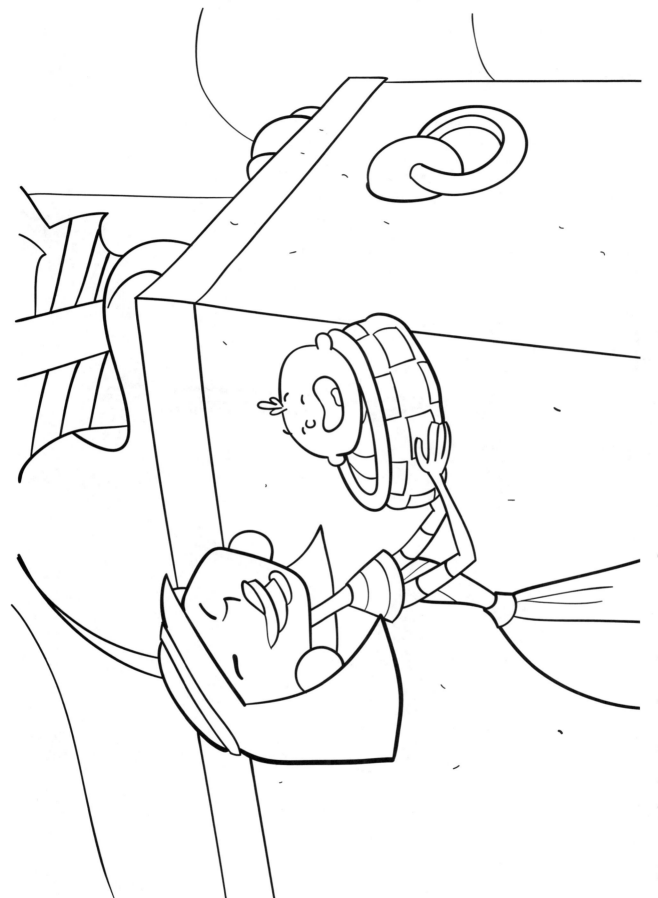

Pharaoh's daughter found the baby Moses in the river and raised him as her own son. He grew up as a prince in Egypt, but ran away to the desert after he defended the Israelites. (Exodus 2)

Moses met his wife, Zipporah, in the desert. (Exodus 2)

God appeared in a burning bush and spoke to Moses, telling him to return to Egypt and free the Israelites from slavery. (Exodus 3)

God told Moses to tell Pharaoh to let the Israelites go. Moses was nervous, but God gave him the words to say! (Exodus 7)

After the pharaoh told Moses that he would not let the Israelites out of slavery, God sent 10 plagues on the Egyptians. Two of those plagues were gnats and frogs. (Exodus 7-12)

For the final plague on Egypt, God told the Israelites to sacrifice a lamb and put its blood on their doors. An angel passed through the town and the firstborn son of all the Egyptian families died, but the firstborn of the Israelite families survived. This was called the Passover. (Exodus 12)

Moses led the Israelites out of Egypt. There were Egyptian soldiers chasing the Israelites when they arrived at the Red Sea. When Moses raised up his staff, God parted the waters and the Israelites walked through safely! (Exodus 14)

Moses and the Israelites went to Mount Sinai. Moses climbed to the top of the mountain, where God came down to give him the Ten Commandments. (Exodus 19)

GOD

God gave Moses the Ten Commandments. (Exodus 20)

When the Israelites reached the Promised Land, Moses sent 12 spies into Canaan.
But 10 of them said the Canaanites were too big and scary.
Because the Israelites did not trust God, he sent them back into the desert. (Numbers 13)

Moses gave a speech that reminded the Israelites to follow God.
That speech is now the whole book of Deuteronomy.

"You shall love the LORD your God with all your heart and with all your soul and with all your might."

Deuteronomy 6:5

JERICHO

The Israelites crossed the Jordan River into the Promised Land, but had to fight for it! They started in Jericho where God knocked the walls down around the city after the Israelites marched around it. (Joshua 6)

The Twelve Tribes of Israel

Joshua reminded the Israelites to give thanks to God and to follow his rules - especially to not bow down to any other gods. (Joshua 23)

"Be strong and courageous. Do not be frightened, and do not be dismayed, for the LORD your God is with you wherever you go."

Joshua 1:9

 whatsinthebible.com

JUDGES

OTHNIEL

EHUD

SHAMGAR

JAIR

JEPHTHA

IBZAN

Here are six of the twelve judges who led the Israelites
back to God when they started to worship other gods.

JUDGES

DEBORAH

GIDEON

TOLA

ELON

ABDON

SAMSON

Here are six of the twelve judges who led the Israelites
back to God when they started to worship other gods.

The Israelites were caught in the cycle of apostasy! They would stop worshipping God, worship fake gods, then they would be in trouble and call out to God! God would send a judge to free the Israelites from their enemy. (Judges)

Ruth was an Israelite woman who promised her mother-in-law Naomi that she would take care of her, even after Ruth's husband died. (Ruth 1)

MOAB

"For where you go
I will go,
and where you lodge
I will lodge.
Your people
shall be my
people, and
your God
my God."

Ruth 1:16

Ruth and Naomi moved to Israel, where Ruth collected grain in a field. (Ruth 2)

Ruth gathered grain in the field of a man named Boaz, who learned how Ruth was taking care of Naomi. Boaz married Ruth! Their son Obed was the grandfather of King David. (Ruth 3-4)

ISRAEL GETS A KING
1 & 2 Samuel

SAMUEL

Samuel was the last of Israel's judges, and he was also a prophet!
God gave Samuel the important task of finding and helping the king of Israel.
(1 Samuel 8:19-22)

The Israelites wanted a king, so God asked Samuel to crown the first king of Israel - King Saul. (1 Samuel 9)

King Saul was very proud of his accomplishments! But he didn't always listen to God, and God sent a new king for Israel. (1 Samuel 15)

Samuel anointed a boy named David to be king after Saul, who became too proud and had forgotten to give all the glory to God. (1 Samuel 16)

"For the LORD sees not as man sees: man looks on the outward appearance, but the LORD looks on the HEART."

1 Samuel 16:7

David fought Goliath, the giant from the Philistine army, and defeated him with just a slingshot and a stone. (1 Samuel 17)

After he beat Goliath, David became popular with the people of Israel! Saul was jealous, and he tried to chase David out of town. Saul and his army chased David for eight years, before Saul died and David became king. (1 Samuel 23:15-28)

David became king of Israel and God promised him that someone
from his family would rule over God's people forever
(the Davidic Covenant). (2 Samuel 7)

David got into trouble with God when he took another man's wife - Bathsheba.
He repented (asked forgiveness) of his sin, but there were still consequences.
Their first son died and another tried to kill David. But their son
Solomon was a great king! (2 Samuel 11)

When David & Bathsheba's son Solomon became king, God appeared to him in a dream and said he could ask God for anything. Solomon asked for wisdom. (1 Kings 3)

GOD

| What's in the Bible? COLORING BOOK   © Jellyfish One, LLC   whatsinthebible.com

When Solomon was king, he built a beautiful temple for the Lord in Jerusalem. (1 Kings 6)

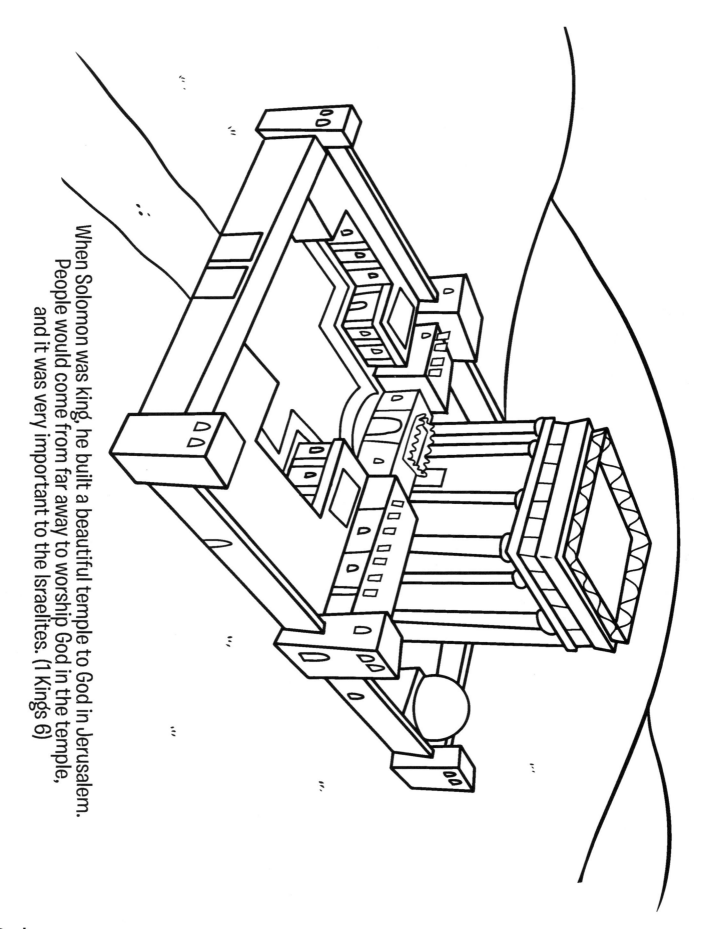

When Solomon was king, he built a beautiful temple to God in Jerusalem. People would come from far away to worship God in the temple, and it was very important to the Israelites. (1 Kings 6)

Solomon's wisdom helped him become rich and famous throughout the world. Then he began to bow to other gods and build huge palaces for his 700 wives. God punished Solomon by splitting the kingdom of Israel in two. (1 Kings 11)

 whatsinthebible.com

Jeroboam was in charge of all of Solomon's building projects, and one day a prophet told Jeroboam that he would be next king of Israel! (1 Kings 11:26-40)

Rehoboam became king after his father Solomon died. Rehoboam was foolish and was mean to the Israelites, who then chose Jeroboam to be their king. (1 Kings 12)

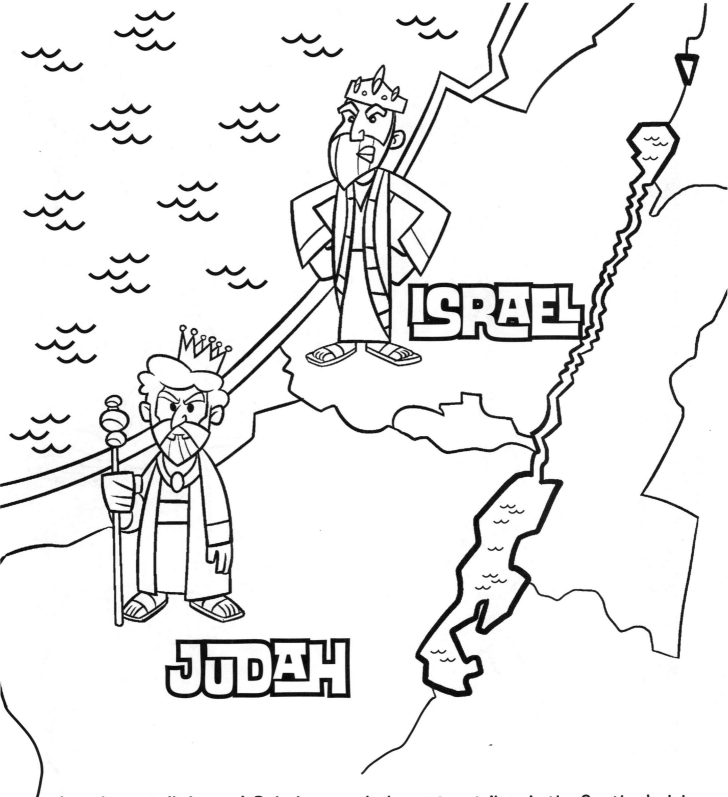

Israel was split in two! Rehoboam ruled over two tribes in the South - Judah and Benjamin - while Jeroboam ruled over the 10 tribes in the North, called Israel.

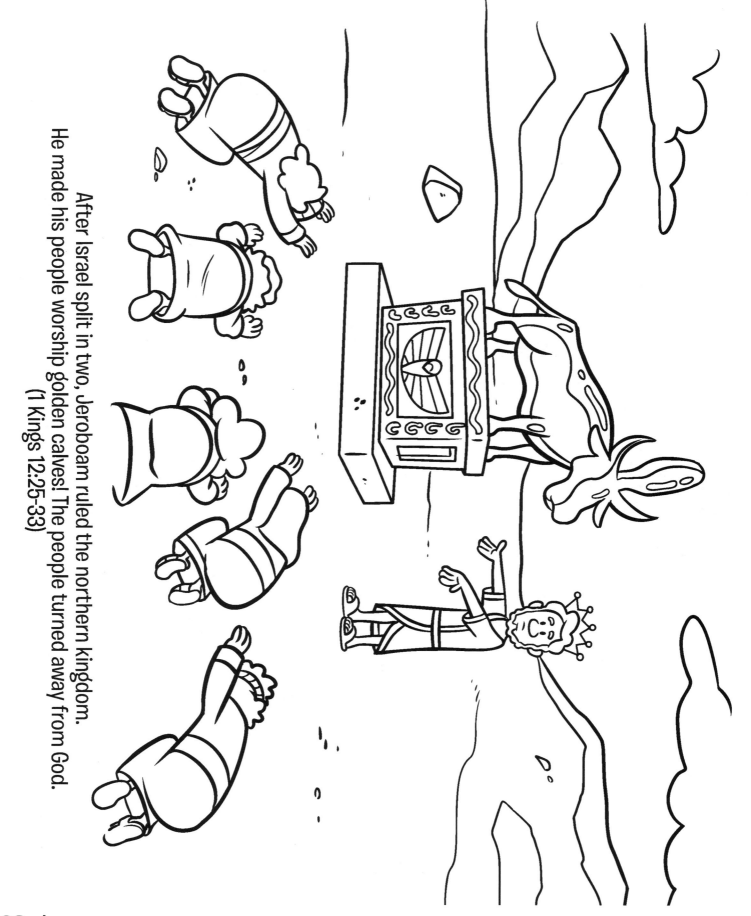

After Israel split in two, Jeroboam ruled the northern kingdom.
He made his people worship golden calves! The people turned away from God.
(1 Kings 12:25-33)

The prophet Elijah had to hide in the wilderness from the evil queen Jezebel. God fed Elijah by sending ravens to bring him bread and meat. (1 Kings 17)

Elijah challenged the prophets of Baal to see whose god would light the sacrifice on fire. When Elijah prayed, the Lord burned up the whole sacrifice! The Israelites were amazed and began to worship the Lord again. (1 Kings 18)

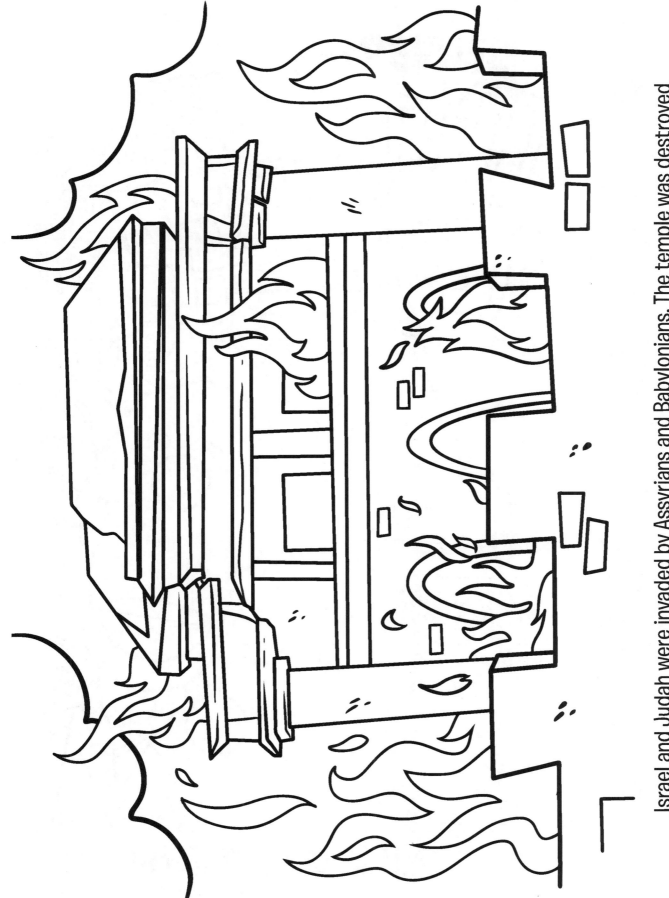

Israel and Judah were invaded by Assyrians and Babylonians. The temple was destroyed and the Israelites were captured and sent to live in Assyria and Babylon. This was called the exile. (2 Chronicles 36:17-21)

God told Isaiah that a king named Cyrus would return the Israelites to Jerusalem, where they would restore the temple. (Isaiah 44:21-28)

Joshua and Zerubbabel led the Israelites to rebuild the temple in Jerusalem, which was finished in 516 BC. (Ezra 3)

King Artaxerxes sent Ezra to Jerusalem to help the Israelites learn God's law again. (Ezra 7)

Nehemiah was the cupbearer to King Artaxerxes, who gave Nehemiah permission to return to Jerusalem and rebuild the city's walls. (Nehemiah 2)

Nehemiah returned to Jerusalem and led the people to rebuild the walls around the city. (Nehemiah 3)

Nehemiah became the governor of the Israelites and Ezra became the priest.

A Jew named Mordecai worked in the palace of King Xerxes. When
Xerxes was looking for a new queen, he chose Mordecai's
cousin Esther. (Esther 2)

Haman was King Xerxes' assistant, and he wanted everyone to bow to him.
When Mordecai refused because of his faith, Haman devised a plan
to kill all of the Jews. (Esther 3)

Esther hosted two dinner parties for Xerxes and Haman. At the second, she revealed that she was Jewish and asked Xerxes to stop Haman from killing her people. Xerxes had Haman killed instead. Esther was a very brave hero! (Esther 7)

VOL. 8

WORDS TO MAKE US WISE

Psalms, Proverbs, & the Writings

Job was a wealthy man who was blessed with many things by God! (Job 1)

Job lost everything - his animals, children, crops - everything except his wife! Job still blessed the Lord, saying "The LORD gave, and the LORD has taken away; Blessed be the name of the LORD." (Job 1)

Job's friends came to visit and told him that he must have done terrible things, which is why he had lost everything. Job said that he had not and that they were terrible friends for not supporting him.

The Lord appeared to Job and his friends in a whirlwind and told them that he rules over all creation with wisdom that they cannot understand. Job realized that God is just and wise and can be trusted, even when bad things happen.

King David wrote many of the Psalms.

"The heavens declare the glory of God, and the sky above proclaims his handiwork."

Psalm 19:1

whatsinthebible.com

"The LORD is my
shepherd;
I shall not want.
He makes me lie down
in green pastures.
He leads me beside
still waters.
He restores my soul."
Psalm 23:1-3

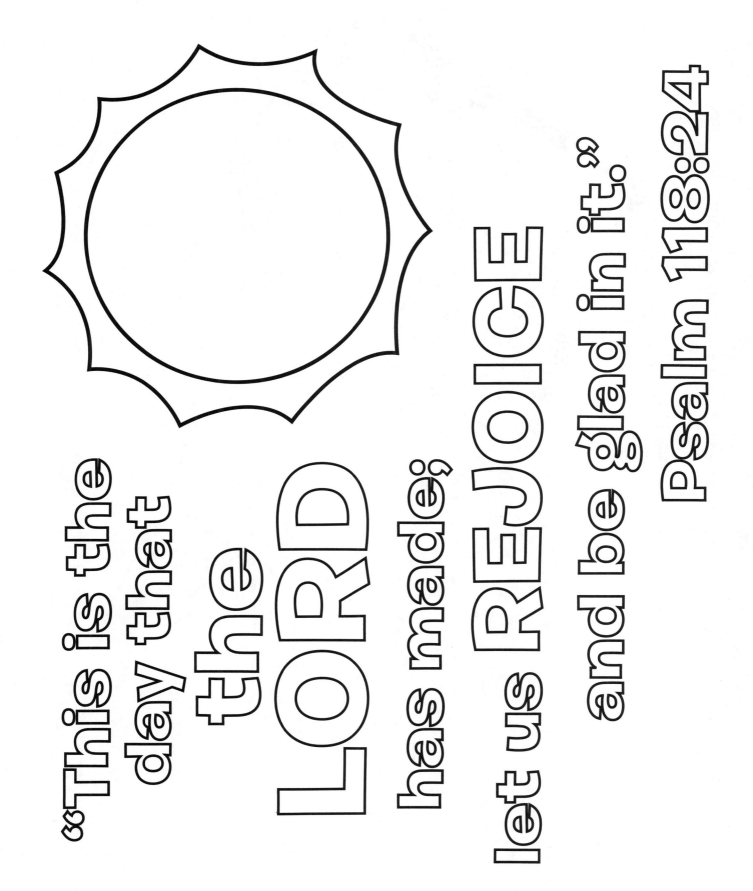

«This is the day that the LORD has made; let us REJOICE and be glad in it.»

Psalm 118:24

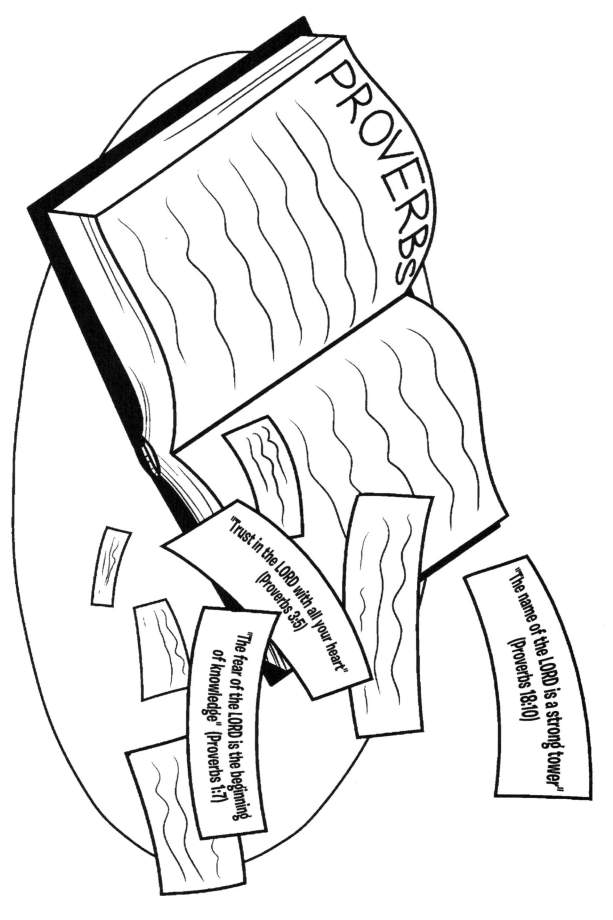

More than 500 of Solomon's wise sayings are recorded in the book of Proverbs.

"Trust in the LORD with all your heart" (Proverbs 3:5)

"The fear of the LORD is the beginning of knowledge" (Proverbs 1:7)

"The name of the LORD is a strong tower" (Proverbs 18:10)

 whatsinthebible.com

"Trust in the LORD with all your heart, and do not lean on your own understanding."

Proverbs 3:5

"The fear of the LORD is the beginning of wisdom."

Proverbs 9:10

Ecclesiastes means "The Preacher." The book of Ecclesiastes is a sermon, possibly given by King Solomon, that talks about the preacher's search for the meaning of life. The preacher knows that true happiness only comes from trusting God and following his commands.

"He has made

EVERYTHING

BEAUTIFUL
in its time."

Ecclesiastes 3:11

The Song of Solomon is a love song between a man and a woman. It is best known for very interesting comparisons - like saying the woman's eyes are like doves, her hair is like a flock of goats and her teeth are like a flock of sheep!

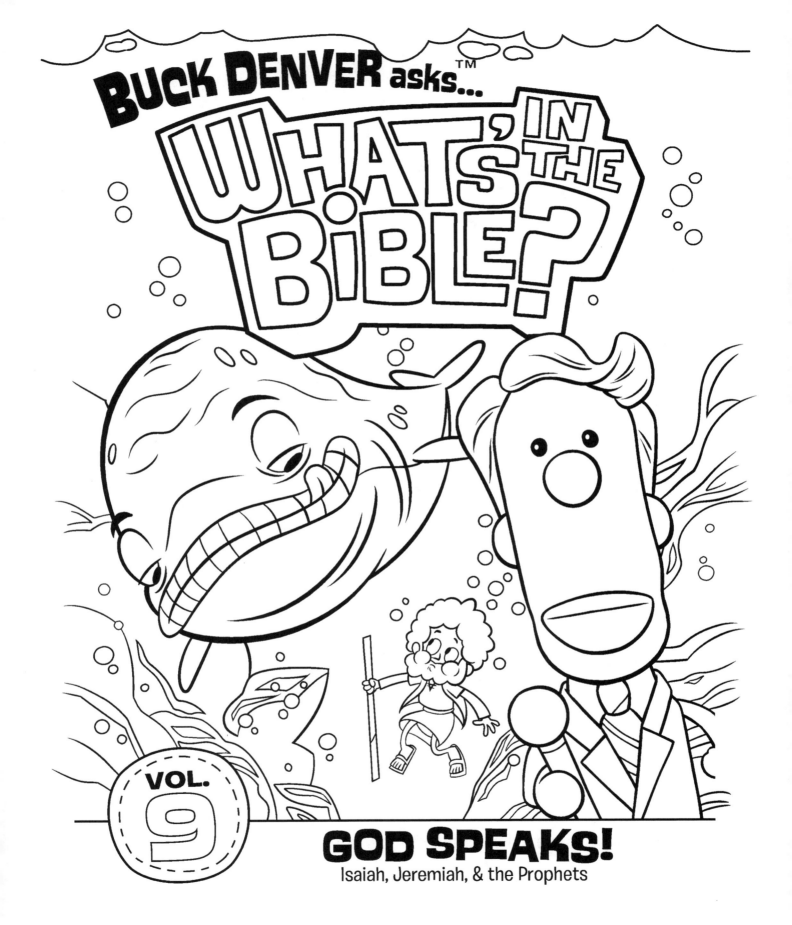

GOD SPEAKS!
Isaiah, Jeremiah, & the Prophets

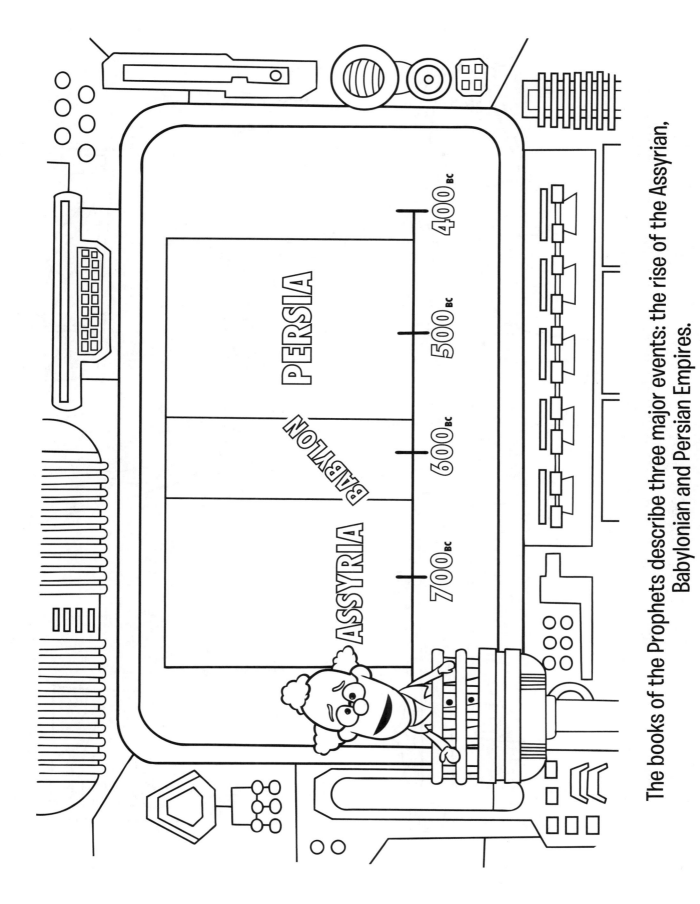

The books of the Prophets describe three major events: the rise of the Assyrian, Babylonian and Persian Empires.

Prophets were kind of like alarm clocks. Prophets would give the Israelites wake up calls when they weren't keeping their promises to God.

ISRAEL

| What's in the Bible? COLORING BOOK   © Jellyfish One, LLC   whatsinthebible.com

ISAIAH

Isaiah was a prophet. God used Isaiah to tell the Israelites
about the Messiah who would come to rescue them!

The prophet Isaiah told King Ahaz to look to God for help when Judah was in trouble, but King Ahaz would not listen. He looked to Assyria for help, but they invaded Judah instead! (Isaiah 7)

GOD

ASSYRIA!

"O LORD, you are my God; I will exalt you; I will praise your name for you have done wonderful things, plans formed of old, faithful and sure." Isaiah 25:1

"Fear not, for I am with you; be not dismayed, for I am your God; I will strengthen you, I will help you, I will uphold you with my righteous right hand."

Isaiah 41:10

"But he was pierced for our transgressions, he was crushed for our iniquities; upon him was the chastisement that brought us peace, and with his wounds we are healed." Isaiah 53:5

The prophet Jeremiah tried to warn the people of Judah for 40 years that trouble was coming, but they chose to listen to false prophets instead.

JEREMIAH

TROUBLE COMING REPENT!

"For I know the plans I have for you, declares the LORD, plans for welfare and not for evil, to give you a future and a hope." Jeremiah 29:11

Ezekiel performed some of his prophecies, and once God told him to show that a siege of Jerusalem was coming by drawing the city on a brick and placing small tents and battering rams around it. Then Ezekiel had to lay next to the tiny city for 390 days! (Ezekiel 4)

King Nebuchadnezzar built a giant idol and asked all the people to bow to it. Three refused - Shadrach, Meshach, and Abednego. Nebuchadnezzar had them thrown into a furnace of fire, but God protected them and they survived! (Daniel 3)

The prophet Daniel interpreted dreams for King Belshazzar. One night, a hand appeared and wrote a message on the king's wall – and Daniel told him it meant that he would not be king much longer! (Daniel 5)

God told the prophet Hosea to marry a woman who kept leaving him, as a way to show the Israelites how painful it was to God when they would turn away from him to start worshipping other gods. (Hosea 3:1)

God told the prophet Jonah to go to Nineveh, but Jonah went the other way - and he ended up in the belly of a whale! After the whale spit him out, Jonah went to Nineveh like God had asked.

"What does the LORD require of you but to do justice, and to LOVE kindness, and to walk humbly with your God?"
Micah 6:8

The prophet Zechariah told the Israelites that they would have a glorious future and that a Messiah would come to save them. (Zechariah 8)

MESSIAH

The prophet Malachi reminded the people to be true to God and remember the covenant that God had made with them - that he would be their God, and they would be his people.

COVENANT

JESUS IS THE GOOD NEWS!

Matthew, Mark, Luke & John

"My soul magnifies the Lord, and my spirit rejoices in God my Savior"

Luke 1:46-47

 whatsinthebible.com

Mary and Joseph traveled to Bethlehem during the census. (Luke 2:1-5)

"For unto you is born this day in the city of David a Savior, who is Christ the Lord." (Luke 2:11)

There were shepherds in the fields near Bethlehem watching their sheep the night Jesus was born. (Luke 2:8-14)

Hark the herald angels sing
"Glory to the newborn King!"

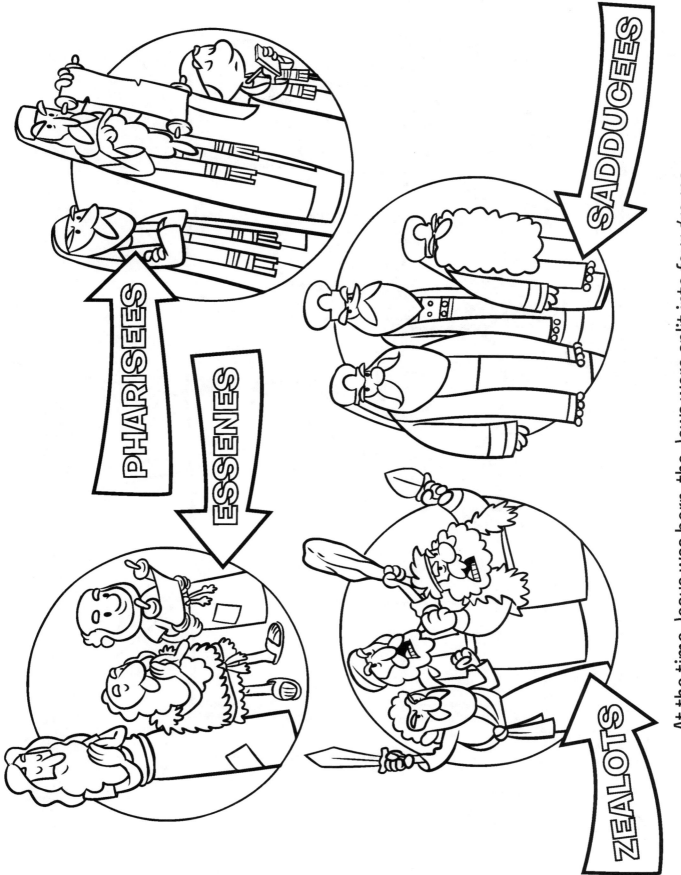

SADDUCEES

PHARISEES

ESSENES

ZEALOTS

At the time Jesus was born, the Jews were split into four groups – Essenes, Pharisees, Zealots, and Sadducees.

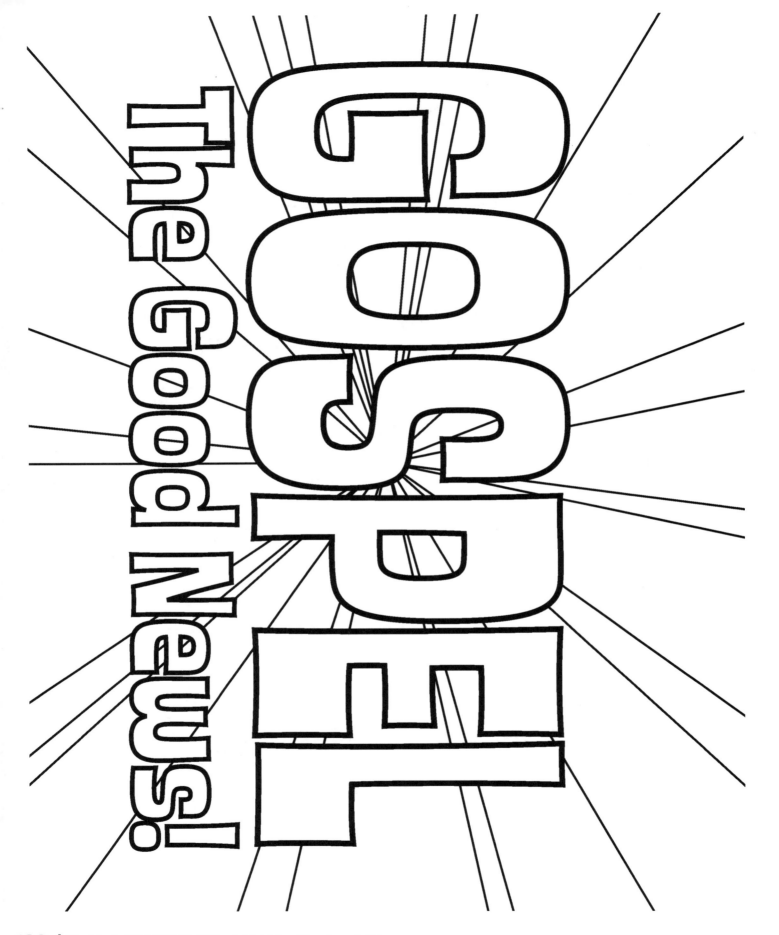

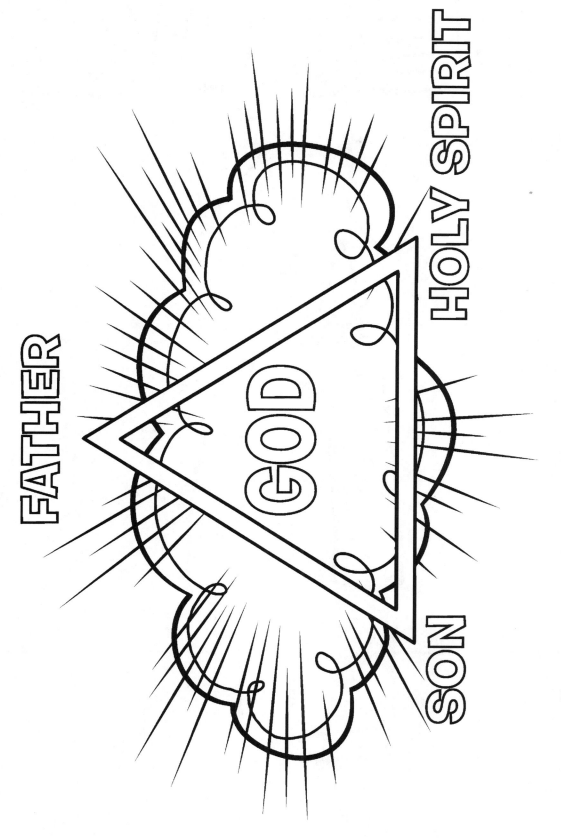

FATHER

HOLY SPIRIT

SON

GOD

There are three persons in the Trinity: the Father, Son and Holy Spirit, but they are all one God.

ABRAHAM

DAVID

JESUS

Jesus came from the line of David and Abraham - fulfilling God's promises to both of them!

John the Baptist was a prophet! He lived in the desert and ate bugs and honey. (Matthew 3)

John baptized Jesus. When he did, the Spirit of God appeared like a dove and a voice from heaven said to Jesus "You are my beloved son." (Matthew 3)

Jesus spent 40 days in the desert, and the serpent came to tempt him. But Jesus used God's words from the Old Testament to stand up to the serpent. (Matthew 4)

Jesus picked 12 men to be his disciples.

Jesus traveled and taught people.
His most famous sermon is called the Sermon on the Mount. (Matthew 5-7)

Jesus performed many miracles, including healing a paralyzed man. (Matthew 9)

"For God so loved the world that he gave his only Son, that whoever believes in him should not perish but have eternal life"

John 3:16

Jesus calmed a storm while he and his disciples were on a boat. (Mark 4:35-41)

"Take my yoke upon you, and learn from me, for I am gentle and lowly in heart, and you will find rest for your souls."

Matthew 11:29

Jesus told parables to teach people about the Kingdom of God. In one famous parable, he said that the Kingdom of God is like a mustard seed - it will start small and then grow! (Mark 4:30-32)

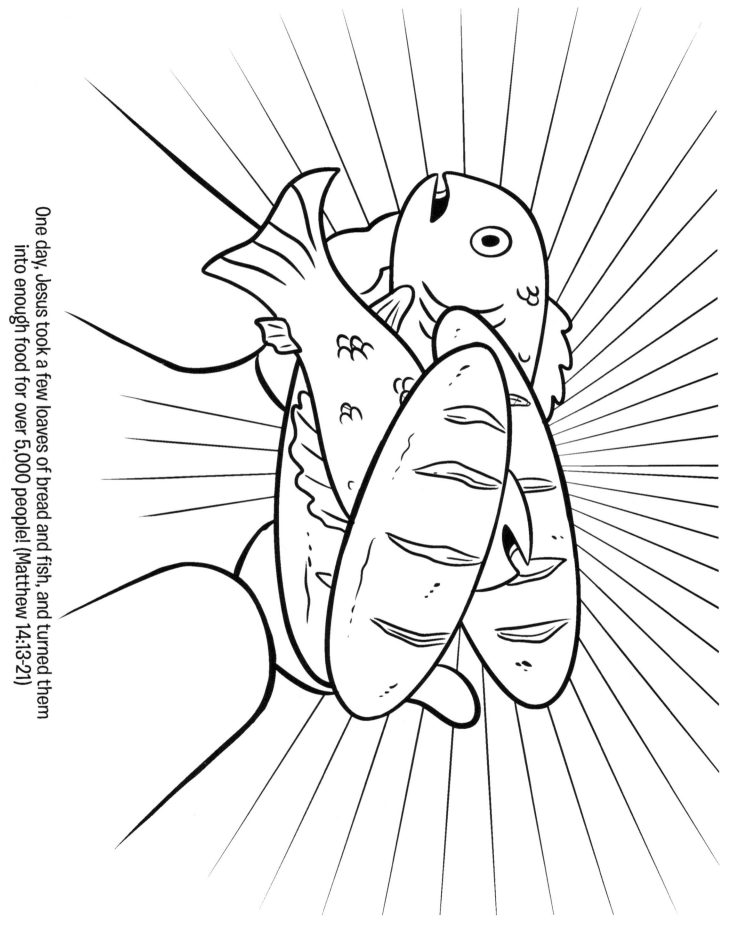

One day, Jesus took a few loaves of bread and fish, and turned them into enough food for over 5,000 people! (Matthew 14:13-21)

"You shall love the Lord your God with all your heart and with all your soul and with all your mind."

Matthew 22:37

Jesus rode into Jerusalem on a donkey and the people cried "Hosanna!" and waved palm branches. (John 12:12-15)

Jesus hosted a Passover meal for his disciples before he died. He told them that his body would be broken and his blood would be shed for them. (Luke 22:14-23)

Jesus prayed in a garden when he knew that he was about to die. He trusted God. (Luke 22:39-44)

One of Jesus' disciples, Judas, betrayed Jesus. Jesus was put on trial and was sentenced to die. (Mark 14:43-50)

Jesus died to save a world that was cursed by sin - he took the punishment for sin, so that all who trust in him could be a part of the Kingdom of God. (Mark 15:33-39)

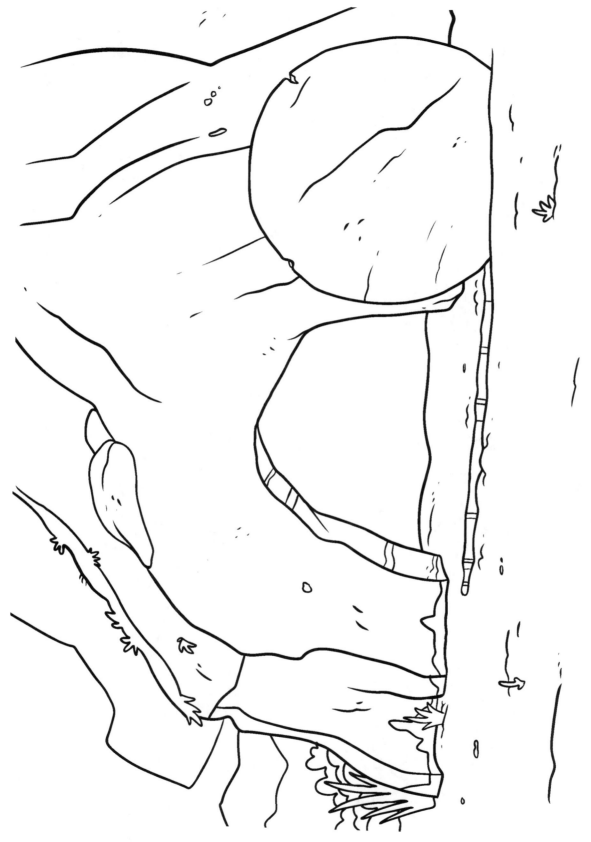

Jesus had been dead for three days when two women went to visit his tomb and found that it was empty. Jesus is risen! He had defeated death. (Mark 16:1-7)

Jesus visited his disciples after he rose from the dead.
He blessed them and went up into Heaven. (Luke 24:36-53)

"GO therefore and make disciples of ALL nations, baptizing them in the name of the Father and of the Son and of the Holy Spirit"

Matthew 28:19

"Let not your hearts be troubled, neither let them be afraid."

John 14:27

SPREADING THE GOOD NEWS!

The Book of Acts

After Jesus appeared to his disciples, he ascended into the clouds. (Acts 1:6-11)

Jesus had promised his followers a special helper – the Holy Spirit! When the Holy Spirit came at Pentecost, he appeared like tongues of fire. (Acts 2)

Jews from all over the world were in Jerusalem for Pentecost, and when the Holy Spirit filled the disciples, everyone was able to understand them in their own language. Many people came to know Jesus when they heard preaching in their own language. (Acts 2:5-12)

Jesus' disciples preached in the temple almost every day, and more and more people became followers of Christ!

The Pharisees and Sadducees didn't like the apostles teaching about Jesus – so sometimes, the apostles were thrown in jail! (Acts 5:17-42)

Stephen was a new believer who taught many people about Jesus. But the Pharisees and Sadducees did not like the preaching of Stephen and Jesus' disciples. Eventually, Stephen was captured and killed for his faith. (Acts 7)

Peter had a dream from God and saw a bunch of animals (that the Jews were forbidden to eat) coming down to him in a sheet. A voice said "get up and eat!" Peter knew that this meant that he was supposed to take the Gospel to everyone - not just the Jews! (Acts 10)

Peter preached the Gospel to a Gentile named Cornelius, and Cornelius' whole household became followers of Jesus! (Acts 10)

Paul was a really mean Pharisee who tried to put all the Christians in prison. (Acts 8)

Paul was on his way to Damascus when Jesus appeared to him and Paul was temporarily blinded! Paul believed in Jesus and became a Christian who taught about Jesus all over the Roman World. (Acts 9)

Paul preached the Good News in Jerusalem and in many other cities around the Roman World, and many people became followers of Jesus.

Members of the early church gathered together regularly to eat and listen to teaching. (Acts 20:7)

Paul traveled to many parts of the Roman World to teach and help start churches. Then he would leave to go to a new town, but he would write letters to the churches to answer their questions and encourage them to keep following Jesus.

Paul wrote 13 letters that are in the New Testament: Romans, 1 & 2 Corinthians, Galatians, Ephesians, Philippians, Colossians, 1 & 2 Thessalonians, 1 & 2 Timothy, Titus, and Philemon.

"And we know that for those who love God all things work together for good, for those who are called according to his purpose."
Romans 8:28

"REJOICE in hope, be PATIENT in tribulation, be CONSTANT in PRAYER."

Romans 12:12

"May the GOD of HOPE fill you with all JOY and PEACE" Romans 15:13

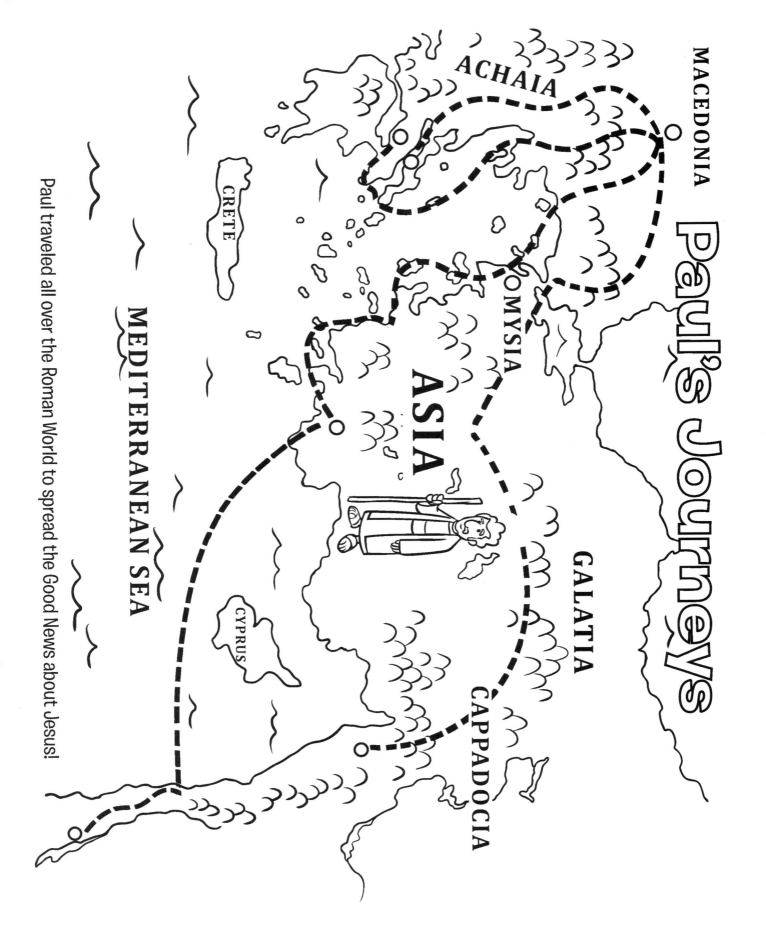

Paul's Journeys

MACEDONIA

ACHAIA

CRETE

MEDITERRANEAN SEA

MYSIA

ASIA

GALATIA

CAPPADOCIA

CYPRUS

Paul traveled all over the Roman World to spread the Good News about Jesus!

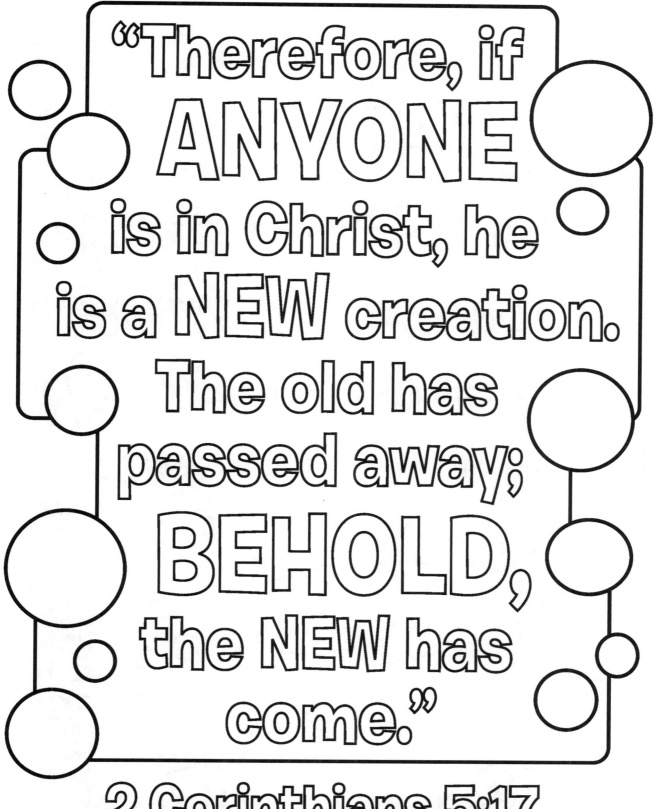

"Therefore, if ANYONE is in Christ, he is a NEW creation. The old has passed away; BEHOLD, the NEW has come."

2 Corinthians 5:17

The Fruit of the Spirit (Galatians 5:22-23)

   whatsinthebible.com

"For by GRACE you have been SAVED through faith. and this is not your own doing; it is the gift of GOD"

Ephesians 2:8

"Do not be anxious about ANYTHING"

Philippians 4:6

"Put on then, as GOD'S chosen ones, HOLY and beloved, compassionate hearts, kindness, humility, meekness, and patience"

Colossians 3:12

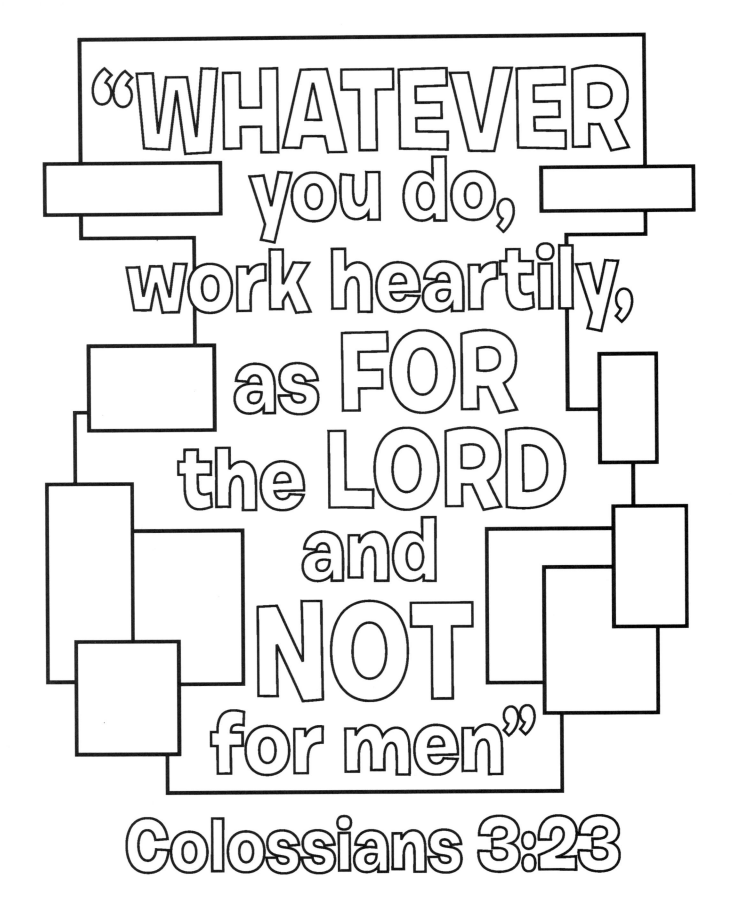

"WHATEVER you do, work heartily, as FOR the LORD and NOT for men"

Colossians 3:23

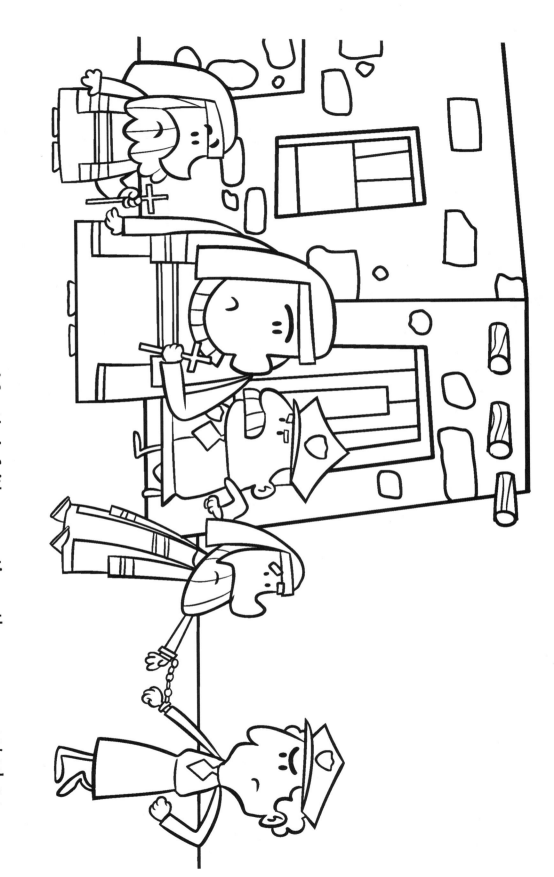

The new Christians were persecuted for their faith – sometimes they were arrested, or their houses were taken away! The book of Hebrews was written as an encouragement to Christians, and we can also be encouraged by its message today.

"Now faith is the assurance of things hoped for, the conviction of things not seen."

Hebrews 11:1

The apostle John was imprisoned on an island called Patmos, where he saw a vision from God that became the book of Revelation.

The book of Revelation is full of symbols! Reading it is like a puzzle – you can find clues to its meaning through the whole Bible. Some of the symbols used in Revelation are seven letters, a scroll with seven seals, seven trumpets, and seven bowls of wrath.

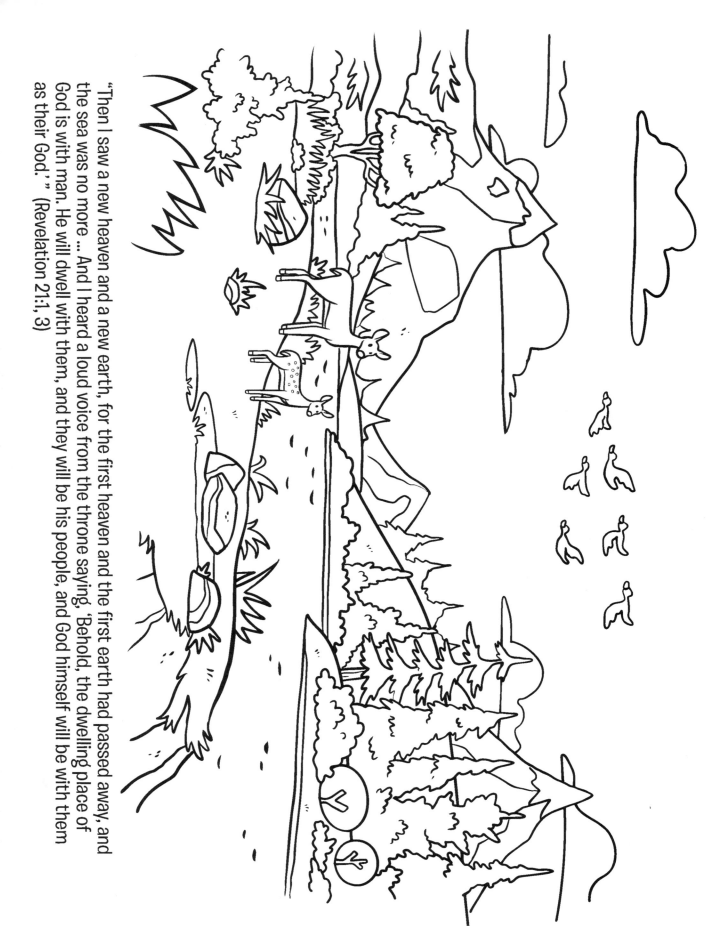

"Then I saw a new heaven and a new earth, for the first heaven and the first earth had passed away, and the sea was no more ... And I heard a loud voice from the throne saying, 'Behold, the dwelling place of God is with man. He will dwell with them, and they will be his people, and God himself will be with them as their God.'" (Revelation 21:1, 3)

CHUCK WAGGIN

MARCY

CAP'N PETE

BROTHER LOUIE

What's in the Bible? COLORING BOOK   © Jellyfish One, LLC   whatsinthebible.com

PASTOR PAUL

CHESTER WHIGGET

BUCK DENVER & FRIENDS™ PRESENT...

SING THROUGH THE BIBLE

INCLUDES 30 BIBLE SING-ALONGS!

WENDELL

JellyTelly.com

What's in the Bible? COLORING BOOK   © Jellyfish One, LLC   whatsinthebible.com

ARMOR UP!

Play the Armor Up! Game at JellyTelly.com

the WONDERFUL WORLD of SCIENCE with Dr. Schniffenhousen

Watch the Wonderful World of Science with Dr. Schniffenhousen at JellyTelly.com!

INDEX

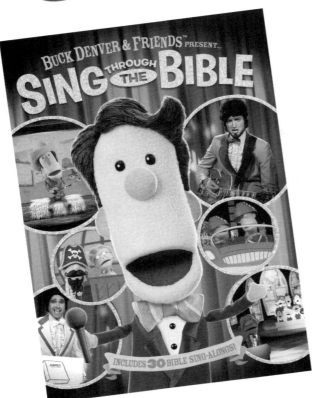

ESV BIBLES FOR KIDS
FROM CROSSWAY

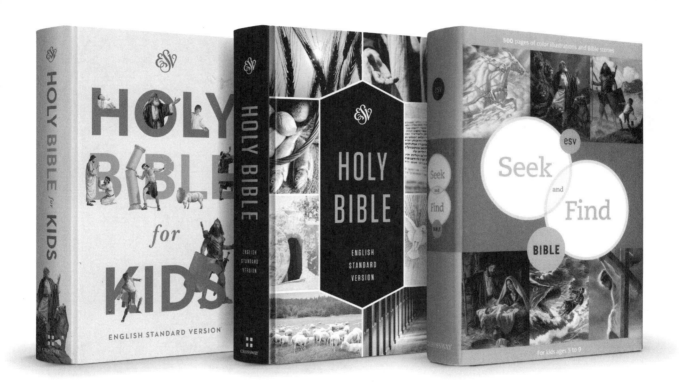

ESV HOLY BIBLE FOR KIDS

ESV HOLY BIBLE TEXTBOOK EDITION

ESV SEEK AND FIND BIBLE

:: CROSSWAY | crossway.org • ESVBible.org